SMITHS at SEA

THE TRUE STORY OF THE SMITH BROTHERS ADVENTUROUS ATLANTIC CROSSING

TOLD BY STANLEY SMITH

Introduction

To a sane man the North Atlantic does not seem to be a place for small boats. However, it calls, and some of us wake up somewhere in the middle. This is a story of what can happen. I include the pictures to prove it.

The Nova Espero is 16 feet waterline length; she is 20 feet over all, 6 feet 3 inches beam, and draws 2 feet 10 inches. She is a gunter-lug rigged sloop, has an ordinary open cockpit, but, in order to make her sea-worthy, we built a 7 foot pram dinghy and lashed it upside down over this with inch and a half manila rope to form a cabin. When all the stores, water and equipment were aboard, we had a space 6 feet long by 4 feet wide in which to live, our headroom was about 3 feet 6 inches.

She was designed by my brother and me on board the Aquitania as we sailed out to Canada in February, 1949, was built by us in Halifax, and, as soon as she was completed, we sailed from Dartmouth, Canada, to Dartmouth, England, without trials, owing to lack of capital. Also, through the same lack,

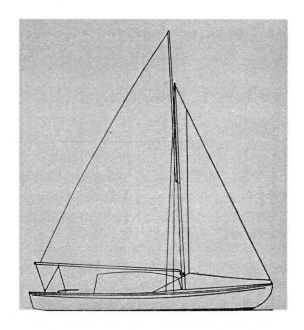

we sailed without a proper sea-anchor, without a chronometer, without a log, without oil-bags, without oilskins, but not without hope!

My undying gratitude is due to my brother and shipmate who contended so serenely with both the dark moods of the Atlantic and my own. Deep thanks also to all these who made us feel so welcome home.

AUTOGRAPHED BY

Foreword by Colin R. Smith

As the 'brother' often referred to in "Smiths at Sea" I have often been asked - as was Stan - 'Why on earth did you do it?' A difficult question, to which I will try to give our reasons as briefly as possible.

Both Stan and I spent some time in Canada during the war (but not together) doing our RAF flying training in order to obtain our pilot's wings. We liked Canada and its people, so much that we decided that we would return as immigrants after the war. So, after demob we pooled most of our service gratuities to buy an old 15 ton, 45 foot gaff cutter in which we planned to sail back to Canada. However, we gave up that idea when *Cerise* developed a bad leak during a cruise down Channel. We managed to make it into Plymouth where we re-caulked the leak and sailed on back to Yarmouth. *Cerise* was now put up for sale and Plan 2 put into operation.

As Stan explains in his *Introduction*, we shipped out on the Aquitania to Halifax, Nova Scotia where we planned to set up our own boat building business. Why, though, would sea-faring Nova Scotians want to buy boats from a couple of unknowns? The answer, of course, was to make ourselves known; demonstrating our confidence in our little boats by a double Atlantic crossing.

Yes, that was the original intention, but not for a moment had it occurred to us that an incredible reception in England (and particularly at Yarmouth, I.W.) would be such as to disrupt, and in my case rule out, a return to Canada. Stan eventually did do so after several years with Charles Violet - and with the addition of a coach-roof on Nova Espero. Their book, *The Wind Calls the Tune*, tells the story. But as to the first crossing - was it crazy? just plain daft? I don't know, but I do know that the memory of it has given me a lifetime of satisfaction and not a moment of regret.

Colin R. Smith, July 2006

Note from the publisher

Since posting the story of my uncles' adventures on a website a few years ago, I have received many messages from the sailing fraternity. Among these, the two most frequently asked questions have been "Where can I buy a copy?", and simply "Why…?".

It's a real pleasure, therefore, to help answer both questions - the latter with many thanks to Colin Smith for his invaluable new foreword.

Robin Somes, July 2006

Smiths at Sea

ONE fine summer day in 1947 my brother Colin and I decided we would like to go to Canada, where wood is plentiful, there to build a "perfect" little sailing boat to sail back across the North Atlantic to England.

Nearly two years later we boarded the Cunard ship Aquitania, bound for Halifax in Canada. We had a nice little cabin, which seemed about 100 feet above sea-level. There were two snug little sleeping-bunks and just enough room to lay out paper and things for designing our boat on the voyage across.

A few hours after leaving Southampton we went to our cabin and settled down quietly to our work. By the time we reached the other side the Nova Espero was ready to build.

We settled down quietly to our work

It was spring when we arrived, although there were no visible signs of this. We had very little money and knew no one at all, so felt anxious as we trudged the snow-covered streets from end to end of the city looking for somewhere to live for the next few months.

It was damp in the cellar

We soon found friends however, for Canadians are generous people.

Our next job was to find a place in which to build the boat. This was not easy. Halifax is a very crowded city and every building seemed to be occupied, but eventually we discovered a basement under an old chapel.

Although the place was big enough, there was some uncertainty about our being able to get the boat out when built.

My favourite tool is the adze

The room we rented was a long way from the only door; she would have to be levered and shunted back and forth from one intervening chamber to another. Even the door allowed us but two inches to spare.

My brother's favourite tool is the hammer

All these chambers were underground so there were no windows, our room being furthest from the door, and cut off from this only source of light by butting walls; we had to rely entirely on electric leads.

It was damp in the cellar.

Within a few days we had all our wood and began to build the boat. Despite the difficulties and the discomfort, those were very happy days indeed.

Soon all the moulds were in place and all sorts of struts and

Reluctant to leave the sanctity of her birthplace

strips of wood were nailed together in all directions, so that the boat looked more like a broken basket than anything else.

A boat-builder needs more tools than any other tradesman, I should think, but perhaps the strangest one of them all is the adze. The adze is a kind of axe, only instead of having the head length-wise to the handle, the blade is fitted at right angles. The handle, too, is curved in a most awkward way, and to the beginner the whole arrangement appears to be designed for the purpose of chopping off one's own feet.

Of course, my favourite tool is the adze.

Less than three months later the Nova Espero was ready to go afloat.

With the help of some friends who inadvertently strolled in at the right moment, we wrenched, wiggled and winkled her out into the sunlight, then up a steep slope into the road and on to a lorry.

We gained the impression that she was loth to leave the sanctity of her birthplace.

We put her down as far as we could and waited for the tide to come in and float her.

Many hours later, she was afloat at last!

Sitting in the water like a little sea-bird, she dipped and swayed as if acknowledging the cheers of the admiring crowd.

A proud day for us.

The admiring crowd

Provisioning

Now followed a period of feverish activity. Sails to lace on, rigging to splice, floor-boards to be fitted, hatches to make, painting and varnishing to be done over and over again. Blocks and bolts and eyes, screws, tacks and nails. Strands of marline, hemp and wire, the smell of Stockholm tar and canvas and, pervading all, the odour of seaweed and salt. Hustle and hurry and a thousand things to remember and forget.

The growing realisation that the day of sailing was rapidly approaching, and oh, what pandemonium prevailed during the last few days. The little boat getting lower and lower, in the water as a never-ending procession of people brought stores and provisions down to the end of the stage.

At last came the great day of sailing!

Fervent farewells to all our friends. A thousand small things to put aboard at the last moment. Presents - of which the most useful was a bottle of rum.

Then we sailed across the harbour to Dartmouth, our point of departure. There the Mayor came down to us and presented us with a letter for the Mayor of Dartmouth in Devon. He entertained us at his home, apparently trying to feed us enough food to last us at least halfway across the ocean.

It was dark when we sailed out of the harbour.

Were we sick?

    The first few days were pleasant enough. A faint breeze, fine weather, the stars and moon at night and the sun by day; and fine big heavy seas gently lifting us and as gently letting us fall.

    Were we sick?

    Don't be silly.

Washing up was done over the side

Washing up was done over the side to conserve our water. We left some at Lat. 41° 27' 00" N. Long. 58° 30' 00" W.

But this simply cannot last out at sea. And before we had really got our sea legs we were in the middle of the mother and father of all storms.

I have to confess I was a little worried!!

But, although things were a bit uncomfortable and wet, my fears were quite unfounded.

Sometimes the Nova Espero was completely buried under falling crests, but the head and shoulders of the man at the tiller filled the only opening, so she never became dangerously waterlogged.

A bit wet

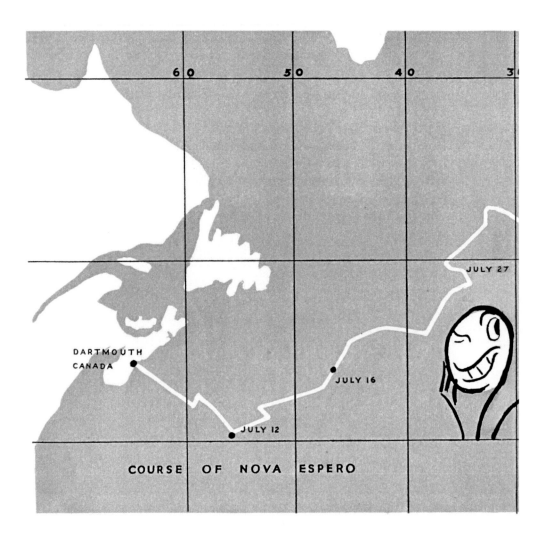

COURSE OF NOVA ESPERO

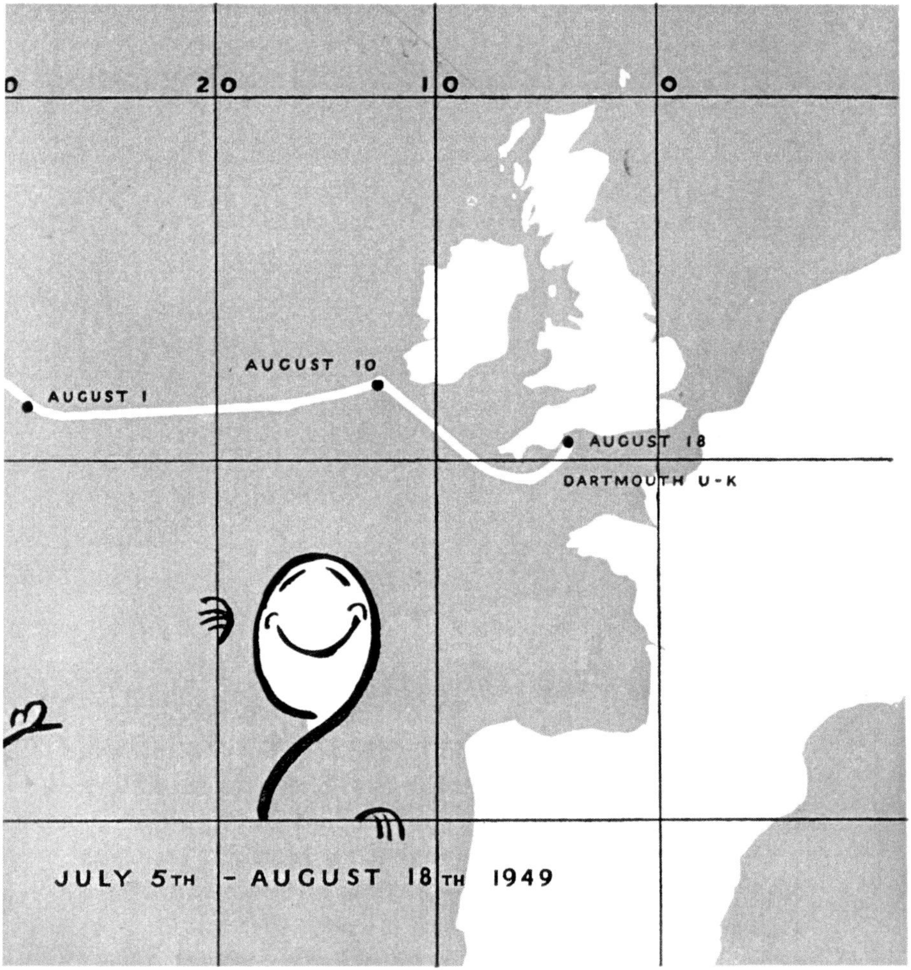

20
10
0
AUGUST 10
AUGUST 1
AUGUST 18
DARTMOUTH U-K
JULY 5TH - AUGUST 18TH 1949

We raised our sterns to let them pass!

All things pass. Storms and breaking seas give way to warm sunshine and dancing wavelets and all is bliss upon the smiling bosom of the ocean - zzzzip, large swordfish pass too.

One sees at the pictures many time the beauteous hero with his waving hair swept sweetly back from his noble brow by the raging wind, his flashing eyes clear to survey the scene.

His waving hair swept sweetly back ?

No matter how heroic I felt, I could never get this effect. The wind persisted in a sort of local down-draught around my head, and I found this most irritating.

We began to feel more inured to the various difficulties. The discomfort of living under the dinghy cabin-top became less acute. The confined space and the continual motion of the boat, which often threw us violently from one side to the other, ceased to annoy us.

Cooking

Wake up, your watch!!

Nevertheless, the ceaseless motion did tend to exhaust us, and I have to admit to a feeling rather difficult to describe when my brother bobbed his head down from the cockpit before dawn to tell me my watch was due.

This sent me sky high

There was another sign that things were wearing me thin. This was my acute sense of pain. I had a large swelling on my hand, and seldom did I come out on deck without some rope end or block giving it a flick. This sent me sky high.

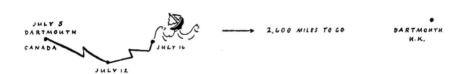

There was one frequent occurrence which always awoke in me a strong sense of injustice: when lying asleep, to be suddenly brought back to life by a bathful of cold sea-water surging down from the cockpit.

Poor porpoise

Still, I was not the only one to receive these unpleasant knocks. We once fell down from a crest right on to a poor porpoise who didn't move quickly enough.

Each day brought us nearer to England, unless a gale of wind drove us back on our track; every day saw my brother "shooting the sun," unless there was no sun; every day another entry in the log, unless I happened to lose the pencil. So it went on day after day, come what weather, our routine: shooting the sun, taking sights, plotting and calculating our position and entering up the log.

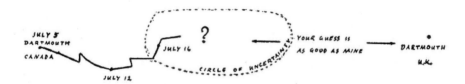

Navigation

Birds!!!

There were many things to interest us, for the Atlantic is not a complete desert by any means.

Birds of many kinds were to be seen. Often we came across a flock of fulmars. These are peculiar, soft-looking birds with shy, winning ways. They do not seem fond of flying like the little stormy petrels which never rest. The only ocean birds we saw fighting and persecuting each other were near the coasts. Other birds we saw were gannets, kittywakes, tern and many more we did not know.

A great part of our time we spent in the Gulf Stream.

The Gulf weed, which comes up from the Sargasso, floats on the surface in little bunches all over the place; we found these to contain the most extraordinary variety of marine life. For the interest of the student of ichthyology, I include a few sketches from memory. I disclaim all responsibility for the accuracy of these.

Little people of the Gulf weed

The friendly enemy

Another interesting creature we saw many times was the Portuguese man-of-war.

This is really a form of co-operative colony.

A large bladder supports it and wears a most beguiling appearance; iridescent colours, with a vane of tiny sails along the back.

But underneath a host of vicious stings awaits the unwary.

Nothing was missing from our trip.
Even whales!
They came up to look at us. Like cows.

One day my brother deserted his post ... but I soon recaptured him.

We sighted about a dozen ships on our way across. But were seen by only three of them; one of these hailed us and we were told: "Another thousand miles, that way."

Out on the broad face of the Atlantic one can commune with nature.

The colours! oh, the lovely, lovely colours of the dawns and sunsets and oh, the clouds. So beeeautiful.

> *Shall my words set forth thy splendourific scene,*
> *The gorgeous feast that there before me spread?*
> *T'would ill bespeak myne ignorific bean,*
> *So, no's the answer. Try your luck instead.*

Marine bard ?

One needn't commune with nature, of course. It's a matter of choice.

Though not much good at thinking, I did sometimes sit there with the most profound thoughts filling my brain, but they always tended to become more and more profound until I was unable to move them. So I could never write them down like a J. B. Priestley.

. . . Sometimes I just sits

One day we sighted a French fishing boat. The crew were very kind and gave us bread and onions and fish. In return for which we gave them a few sticks of black twist chewing tobacco.

Entente Cordiale!!

We finished the rum

At long last after many weary weeks we sighted land. We finished the remaining rum and felt happy.

We did not know what sort of welcome awaited us at Dartmouth, our first port of call: two or three friends perhaps, with a pleasant reunion party. That was all we expected. . . .

But as we neared the harbour entrance, a dainty little white yacht sailed out to greet us: "Where in --- have you been all this time. Have you got a lobster pot in tow?" Our friends. It was a merry thought to come out and escort us into port.

Expectations

Merrythought's greeting

. . . Well, you never know your luck, do you?

All England seemed to have come to Dartmouth to see us sail in. We cowered in the centre of a storm of merry-making and festivity. We were never more frightened in our lives. By the time we had sailed along the coast to Yarmouth in the Isle of Wight, our HOME, we had shrivelled down to two tiny points of

The awesome welcome

embarrassment, grinning sheepishly as we met the gazes of our old school-friends and neighbours.

If England was pleased to see us, we were overjoyed to see our dear old England.

That's all—good night !

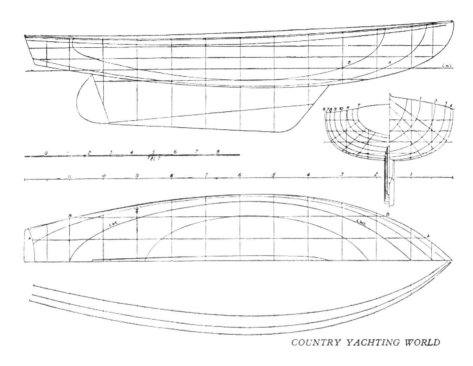

DESIGN OF NOVA ESPERO

The Nova Espero is one of the smallest boats ever to cross the Atlantic Ocean. Her total length overall is 20 ft.; length on the water line 16 ft.; width 6 ft. 3 ins.; draft 2 ft. 10 ins.

Dedicated to Miss Catherine Elisabeth Violet, daughter of my friend and shipmate, Charles Violet.

ISBN 1-904690-43-2

2006 edition published by
Robin Somes
The Cottage, Badminston Drove,
Fawley, Hants., SO45 1BW, UK.
www.badminston.demon.co.uk
www.robinsomes.co.uk

Printed and bound by CPI Antony Rowe, Eastbourne

First published in May 1951 by
ROBERT ROSS & CO LTD
in association with
GEORGE G. HARRAP & CO LTD